Learn from

The Wisdom

of

Luqman

Dr. Muddassir Khan

Bismillahir Rahmaanir Raheem.

In the Name of Allah, The Most Merciful, The Bestower of Mercy.

قُلْ أَعُوذُ بِرَبِّ ٱلنَّاسِ ①

Say, "I seek refuge in (the) Lord (of) mankind,

مَلِكِ ٱلنَّاسِ ② إِلَٰهِ ٱلنَّاسِ ③

(The) King (of) mankind, (The) God (of) mankind,

مِن شَرِّ ٱلْوَسْوَاسِ ٱلْخَنَّاسِ ④

From (the) evil (of) the whisperer, the one who withdraws,

Preface

All praise is due to Allah. We praise Him, seek His assistance and forgiveness and we seek refuge with Him from the evil of our souls and our misdeeds.

I testify that there is no deity worthy of worship except Allah alone. He has no partner. I also testify that Muhammad (peace and blessings of Allah be upon him) is His slave and Messenger.

This is a short book based on the teachings of Shaykh 'Abdurrazzaq al-Badr (Allah have mercy on him).

This book was written for the person who is desirous of becoming a good Muslim. Everyone should read it to gain from the immense wisdom of Luqman. It is especially beneficial for a parent.

This book serves as a source of light in the darkness of sins that surround us. You will learn how to experience true faith when you read this book. This book will not only purify your soul but will also teach you how to escape sins. It contains authentic events, advice, and stories that will inspire you to move to the next level in your journey towards the Hereafter.

If you have been desiring to have a loving relationship with your Lord, then this book is written so that you can achieve this goal with ease.

This is not just a self-help book but is a manual of your journey towards becoming a good Muslim. This book will keep your heart from becoming hard and dark. It is a book of hope and forgiveness. You can heal your heart and improve yourself no matter where you have started this journey. This book can serve as a source of your awakening and returning to the Islamic version of yourself.

By reading this compact but comprehensive book with a pure intention and attentive heart, you can cultivate your love for Allah and the Messenger (peace and blessings of Allah be upon him) and live a life of gratitude and contentment.

A Muslim is encouraged to utter certain phrases at the mention of Allah, the Prophet, other Prophets, the angels, the companions of the Prophet, and righteous Muslims. Please say these phrases whenever you come across them in the book.

Allah: Say *"Subhaanahuu wa ta'aalaa"* which means 'Glorified and Exalted is He.'

Prophet Muhammad: Say, *"Sallallaahu 'alayhi wa salam"* which means, 'May the peace and blessing of Allah be on him.' Say this phrase always when you hear the beloved name of the Prophet or at any place where the Prophet is mentioned.

Other Prophets or an Angel: Say, *"Alayhis Salaam"* which means, 'Peace be on him.'

A male companion of the Prophet: Say, *"Radiyallaahu 'anhum"* which means, 'May Allah be pleased with him.'

A past scholar or righteous Muslim: Say, *"Rahimahullaah"* which means, 'May Allah have Mercy on him.'

A female companion: Say *"Radiyallaahu 'anhaa"* which means, 'May Allah be pleased with her.'

Hadeeth: Actions are but by Intentions

إِنَّمَا الْأَعْمَالُ بِالنِّيَّاتِ،

Actions are but by intentions,

وَإِنَّمَا لِكُلِّ امْرِئٍ مَا نَوَى،

and every man shall have only that which he intended.

فَمَنْ كَانَتْ هِجْرَتُهُ إِلَى اللهِ

Thus he whose migration (Hijrah to Madeenah from Makkah) was for Allah

وَرَسُولِهِ

and His Messenger,

فَهِجْرَتُهُ إِلَى اللهِ وَرَسُولِهِ،

his migration was for Allah and His Messenger,

وَمَنْ كَانَتْ هِجْرَتُهُ لِدُنْيَا يُصِيبُهَا

and he whose migration was to achieve
some worldly benefit,

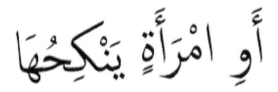

or to take some woman in marriage,

فَهِجْرَتُهُ إِلَى مَا هَاجَرَ إِلَيْهِ

his migration was for that for which he
migrated.

THE PROPHET (PEACE AND BLESSINGS
OF ALLAH BE UPON HIM) SAID:

"MY GREATEST JOY LIES IN PRAYER."

Introduction

Praise is due to Allah. We praise Him, ask for His help, and come back to Him. We seek refuge with Him against the evil of our souls and the harmful consequences of our actions. No one can lead astray him whom Allah has led, and no one can lead him whom he has led astray. I testify that Only Allah is worth worshiping, without an associate, and I testify that Muhammad is His servant and His Messenger.

The recommendations found in Luqman's account contain wonderful teachings, precious counsel, and blessed words. This is a perfect example of how to call to Allah, educate children and train future generations. This dialogue describes effective ways and best practices for calling people to Allah and teaching them good.

Thus, educators, parents as well as teachers must pay particular attention to these recommendations and meditate on them at length in order to derive the best way to teach and call to Islam.
Plus, these recommendations are a great example of wisdom to win hearts and grab attention.

Also, they contain prompts and warnings, good exhortations, and illustrate the proper way to approach people for the purpose of teaching them good and calling them to the religion of Allah.

In fact, preaching is on the one hand a knowledge that is learned and an action that is explained, and on the other hand, it requires wisdom, effective means and touching turns that reach hearts.

Allah granted to His servant Luqman wisdom and placed it in his heart. He made his word, his exhortation, his teaching as a wise counsel.

Most scholars have ruled that Luqman was a sage and not a messenger.

Wisdom requires that we meditate, seek deeply to understand and study the recommendations that Allah has mentioned in His Book, the Noble Quran in Surah Luqman Verses 12 to 19:

We have indeed given Luqman wisdom, (and said) Be grateful to Allah, and whoever is grateful is grateful only for himself. As for him who is ungrateful ... Verily, Allah is Rich, Beyond need, and He is worthy of praise.

And when Luqman said to his son while exhorting him: "O my son, do not give a partner to Allah, for association with [Allah] is truly a huge injustice."

We have commanded man [beneficence and to take care of] his father and mother. His mother carried him [suffering for him] weakness after weakness; his weaning takes place at two years. Be grateful to Me as well as to your parents. Towards Me is the (final) destination.

But if both (parents) force you to associate with Me what you have no knowledge of, then do not obey them; but stay with them here below in a proper way (showing kindness to them). And follow the path of one who turns to Me (in repentance). To Me, then, is your return, and then I will inform you of what you were doing.

(Luqman said), "O my child, were it (a wrong) the weight of a grain of mustard, at the bottom of a rock, or in the heavens or in the earth, Allah will bring it out. Allah is Subtle and Perfectly Knowledgeable (All-Aware).

O my child, complete the prayer, command the proper (enjoin what is right), forbid the blameworthy (wrong), and endure what happens to you with patience. This is one of the firm resolutions!

And do not turn away your face from men (out of pride), and do not tread (walk) the earth with arrogance: for Allah does not love the presumptuous (vain) full of glory (boastful).

Be modest in your approach (walk with a moderate pace), and lower your voice, because the most hated voice is the voice of donkeys."

We can learn a set of lessons from these wise counsels of Luqman.

Lessons from the Luqman story

Lesson 1: Wisdom is a gift from Allah

Wisdom is a divine gift which Allah bestows upon whomever He wills from among His servants, as the following verse (surah Luqman: 12) show us:

"We have indeed given Luqman wisdom."

It is therefore from Allah that wisdom comes. We also find proof of this in the word of Allah:

"He gives wisdom to whomever He wants. And the one to whom wisdom is given, really, it is an immense good which is given to him." (al-Baqarah: 269)

So, whoever wants Allah to grant him this wisdom or any other good, let him ask Allah directly, since good and grace are in His possession. He grants them to whomever He wills, and Allah is the Holder of enormous bounty.

Also, good is only obtained by being sincere towards Him, by turning to Him in a good way, by obeying Him, by asking Him for success by relying totally on Him to obtain it. Indeed, guidance and success can only come from Allah.

Lesson 2: Ways to Obtain Wisdom

Obtaining wisdom requires causes that the servant must implement. Indeed, whoever carefully meditates on Luqman's story and stops for a moment to meditate on his life will find that he was a pious servant, a devotee, who hastened to obey Allah and had a special relationship with his Lord. The scholar Ibn Kathir, as well as other scholars, described him as follows: "He was a devotee, full of fervor for Allah, as well as a truthful person. He spoke little but reflected and meditated a lot. He took advantage of assemblies (gatherings of knowledge) for good and encouraged them to do the same. In addition, he encouraged people to consult and benefit from scholars."

The lesson to be drawn from this is that by implementing the beneficial means which bring closer to Allah, results in good, success and wisdom. It is for this purpose that the Prophet (peace and blessings of Allah be upon him) said, "Strive for what will be profitable for you and seek the help of Allah."

The Prophet (peace and blessings of Allah be upon him) also said, "Knowledge is acquired through learning and good manners only through self-control (patience). Whoever strives to seek good will obtain it, and whoever seeks to protect themselves from evil will be preserved from it."

Therefore, it is essential to carry out the means which make it possible to obtain wisdom. It is not enough to ask Allah for wisdom, beneficial knowledge and good deeds without achieving the necessary causes.

Allah said:

"It is You Alone that we worship, and it is You Alone whom we implore for help." (al-Fatiha: 5)

"So worship Him and place your trust in Him." (Hud:123)

Lesson 3: The need to be grateful for the bounties of Allah, and the fact that this causes their preservation, improvement and increase

Indeed, Allah has said about this:

"We did give Luqman wisdom, (and said) 'Be grateful to Allah.'"

So whenever a blessing is received through gratitude, it will endure. Otherwise, it will disappear. This is the reason why certain scholars have qualified recognition (of the blessing from Allah - gratitude) as "protective" and "preservative" since it preserves both existing benefits and arouses the appearance of new favors.

Allah affirmed:

"If you are grateful, most certainly I will increase [My benefits] for you." (Ibrahim: 7)

He commanded Luqman: "Be grateful to Allah."

That is to say: be grateful to Him for the blessings, generosity and honors that He has given you.

Indeed, Allah satisfied this pious servant by granting him beneficial wisdom and knowledge. Likewise, He enabled him to do good deeds. There is therefore evidence in this which shows that when Allah grants knowledge and good actions to His servant, he must constantly show gratitude to Him by acknowledging His grace and His guidance.

Lesson 4: How to be grateful

The recognition of a benefit is expressed through the heart, the tongue and actions. These three forms of gratitude are all covered by the word of Allah: "Be grateful to Me."

One to whom wisdom, beneficial knowledge, and righteous deeds have been bestowed must show gratitude to Allah [in three ways]:

- By the heart: by recognizing His benefit in his heart.
- By the tongue: by celebrating the praises of Allah, by glorifying Him and by thanking Him.
- By the body: by using this benefit in His obedience.

As He revealed:

"O family of David! Work out of gratitude." (Saba: 13)

For the servant it is a question of doing good deeds and of being quick to obey. It is also about making sure to use these blessings in the ways that Allah has commanded to follow.

Lesson 5: Recognition of the servant (Gratitude) is of no benefit to Allah - Allah is Rich, Beyond any need

The gratitude of grateful people does not benefit Him, and the denial of ungrateful does not harm Him, as He Himself has declared:

"Be grateful to Allah, and whoever is grateful, is grateful only for himself. As for him who is ungrateful ... Verily, Allah is Rich, Beyond need and He is worthy of praise."

The obedience of those who obey Allah or the gratitude of those who are grateful to Him do not benefit Him; and neither their ingratitude nor their disobedience does Him any harm.

Besides, meditate on this in the hadith Qudsi in which Allah says: "O My servants! If all the men and jinn, from the first to the last of you, had a heart as good as the best man among you, it would not increase My kingship in any way. O My servants! If all men and jinn had a heart as bad as the worst man among you, it will not diminish My kingdom."

This hadith therefore confirms what has just been mentioned above.

Allah also says:

"Whoever takes the right path takes it only for himself; and whoever goes astray, only goes astray at his own expense." (al-Isra: 15)

Allah, Himself, is the possessor of all wealth and is worthy of praise.

Along the same lines, He said:

"O men, you are the needy in need of Allah, and it is Allah who is the rich, Free of any need, and He is the One to be praised. If He wanted He would make you disappear, and bring up a new creation."

Lesson 6: Recognizing Benefit (Gratitude) Affects the Servant

The gratitude of the servant for the beneficence of Allah is a good deed, the consequences and benefits of which are profitable to the servant.

"Whoever is grateful is not grateful but for oneself (for his own benefit)."

If the servant shows gratitude, this action will benefit him in this world and in the Hereafter. In this lower world, this will result in the preservation and sustainability of this blessing, and in the gain of other graces, as previously mentioned. In the Hereafter, this will result in reward, retribution, and a happy ending. So when the servant shows appreciation, that gratitude will benefit him and him alone. It is for this purpose that Allah said: "Whoever takes the right path takes it only for himself; and whoever goes astray, goes astray only to his own detriment."

On the other hand, if the servant is ungrateful for the blessing with which he has been blessed - May Allah preserve us - his ingratitude will be for him a misfortune and a source of regret and remorse both here in this world and in the Hereafter.

The servant must become aware of this reality, that is to say of the fact that it is he who is in the need to show himself to be grateful to Allah, whereas Allah does not need the recognition (gratitude) of His servant.

Lesson 7: Be convinced that Allah needs absolutely nothing but His creation need Him totally

Allah said: "Verily, Allah is Rich, beyond need, and He is worthy of praise."

We firmly believe that Allah is "Al-Ghaniy". This attribute is one of His sublime names. Indeed, Allah is unlike His creation who are entirely dependent on Him in every way. Also, we believe that our Lord has ascended and established himself on His throne, and that He is different from His creatures, as He has informed us in the verses:

"The Most Gracious Has Established Himself on the Throne."

"Then He established Himself on the Throne."

At the same time, we have the firm belief that Allah is also free of need for His throne and all that is below, but that the whole of creatures - that is, His Throne and all that is below - are in greatest need of Allah:

"Allah holds back the heavens and the earth so that they do not collapse. And if they sag, no one after Him can hold them back. He is Forbearing and Forgiving."

It is therefore Allah who holds back His throne, who holds back the heavens and the earth. And all of His creatures live only by His permission. They cannot do without Him even for a moment.

Lesson 8: The Affirmation that Allah holds all the attributes of perfection worthy of praise

It is about believing that Allah deserves the most perfect praise, because of His praiseworthy and perfect names.

"To Him is (due all) praise here in the first (life) and in the hereafter."

All praise goes to Him from start to finish. And to Him is gratitude, both inwardly and outwardly since all blessings come from Allah. There is no favor without it coming from Him. It is therefore for Him that praise should be expressed.

Allah said:

"As for him who is ungrateful ..., Verily, Allah is Rich, beyond need, and He is worthy of praise."

"Al-Hamid" is one of the beautiful names of Allah. It indicates that Allah is constantly praised and entitled to be so, whatever the time and circumstances. Thus, He is praised because of His names and attributes as well as for the graces He bestows on His servants. Indeed, He possesses all the praiseworthy qualities and to Him all the praise:

Lesson 9: The Benefits of Wisdom

These verses in the Quran about Luqman illustrate the importance of wisdom and its immense usefulness to the one whom Allah has favored by bestowing it on him. This is evident in this blessed account, by the fact that Allah praised Luqman and praised him for the fact that He gave him wisdom. And this makes the servant wonder what wisdom is while seeking to adorn himself with that character.

This notion has been defined in different ways:

- Some have said that wisdom is none other than beneficial knowledge followed by good deed.

- Other people of knowledge have said that it is wisdom to put things in their respective places.

- It has also been described as prophecy, understanding, correctness in speech and wise opinion.

- Others have explained it differently.

The main thing to remember is that wisdom is of paramount importance, and that it is up to every servant to strive to acquire it by using the legislated means which make it possible to obtain it.

Lesson 10: The Importance of Exhortation (admonishment) as a Method of Education and Teaching

Allah said, "And when Luqman said to his son while urging him."

Indeed, the way of exhorting has a huge impact on the education of people and the teaching of children. According to scholars, exhortation is a knowledge that is transmitted and that one advises to apply, accompanied by encouragement and / or warning. For the exhorter, it is a question of mentioning the good while stating the benefits which flow from it, and vice versa.

In short, the exhortation is both an order to do good and a prohibition against doing evil using forms of incitement and deterrence.

The inducement consists in mentioning the generated benefits, consequences and positive effects which flow from a desirable act performed by the servant. Conversely, the warning consists in mentioning the dangers and damage caused by the performance of a prohibited act.

It is therefore in this way that Luqman the Wise proceeded by including in his recommendations, a beneficial incentive which encourages his son to perform the action in the best possible way, as well as a convincing warning. which dissuades him from approaching sin and committing a crime.

Lesson 11: The importance of tenderness and gentleness with the one who receives advice or teaching and their decisive impact

In fact, when you want to exhort and advise a person, it is welcome to show tenderness towards him by using sweet words and elegant terms that will make your word reach his heart and that it opens to him and listen to you. Note here that, Luqman, while exhorting his own son, used beautiful words poignantly expressed, going straight to the heart. Likewise, observe his delicacy in the exhortation addressed to his son: you will find the expression "O my son!" which has been repeated several times in the story given the impact it has on the heart and morale of the child. In addition, it encourages him to pay full attention so that he can fully benefit from this exhortation, especially if it is expressed gently.

On the other hand, when the exhortation is empty of tenderness - as when a person who wants to advise or forbid says to his son rudely: "O boy" before advising him. Or name him by animal names as happens in some people who wish to exhort or warn their child - how can the heart of the person being counseled open to this kind of speech, which has the consequence of inciting even more to close oneself and to be stubborn?!

There is therefore a profound difference between this manner and the one used gently, like the words of Luqman "O my son!" Full of tenderness, compassion, fatherly instinct and mercy, which made his heart open.

In addition, admire the gentleness used in the story of Mu'adh Ibn Jabal (Allah be pleased with him) when one day, the prophet (peace and blessings of Allah be upon him) took him by the hand and said, "O Mu'adh! I love you!

- Mu'adh answered him: "O Messenger of Allah! You are dearer to me than my father and mother! I love you too."

- Then he added: " O Mu'adh! I make a recommendation to you: do not forget to say at the end of each prayer: "O Allah! Help me to call on You (remember You), to be grateful to You and to worship You in a good way!"

He (peace and blessings of Allah be upon him) first began with gentleness and compassion so that Mu'adh's heart opened deeply and in order to encourage him to receive the teaching.

This is therefore essential when one calls to Allah and teaches good.

Lesson 12: Respect Priorities in Preaching

Indeed, it is appropriate for parents, educators and those who call to Allah to pay some attention to this when calling people to good. We must start with the most important and so on, even in the education of children and future generations.

We begin by anchoring the bases of healthy dogma and good belief. Then we teach the different worship, good manners and noble behavior. We find that when the Prophet (peace and blessings of Allah be upon him) sent Mu'adh ibn Jabal to Yemen, he said, "You're going to a people among the People of the Book. May the first thing you call them is that they worship none other than Allah, the Most Exalted."

This is what Luqman the wise did. When he wanted to make a set of recommendations beneficial to his son, he began by saying: "O my son, do not associate with Allah", out of respect for the orders of priority.

Lesson 13: Polytheism is the worst of all sins

And it is the most dangerous and the one against whom Allah warned the most. This is deduced from the fact that Luqman began by warning his son about the worst of things, and this is the way people of good advice proceed who, when they want to forbid bad things, start with the most dreadful. It is for this reason that Luqman began by forbidding polytheism to his son.

Also, we will notice that in this noble context, that he forbade him several things, including pride, naivety, arrogance but the first thing he forbade is the Shirk, which shows that this act is the most nefarious and the most destructive of sins.

Lesson 14: The Importance of Educating Children by Teaching Them Pure Monotheism

We deduce this from his recommendation: "O my son, give no partner to Allah."

Children indeed need, from an early age, to be warned against polytheism and to be invited to pure monotheism ("Tawhid") and to dedicate their worship exclusive for Allah. Therefore, if one teaches to the child oneness of Allah from an early age, then by Allah's permission, it will be of great benefit to him.

This is also one of the wisdoms in naming one's children Abdullah and Abdurrahman [as was reported in the following hadith: "The best names are Abdullah and Abdurrahman"]. These names will teach the child to remain on monotheism and keep it in his mind that he is only the servant of Allah, and not the slave of his impulses, nor of this lower world, nor of Satan, nor of his inciting soul to evil. From then on, the child will develop according to the foundations of faith and the bases of belief, which are the foundations on which religion and legislation are built.

However, faith is only valid if it is based on the oneness of Allah and His exclusive worship.

Lesson # 15: Association of partners with Allah is a huge injustice

The *Shirk* (associating partners with Allah and worshipping them) is the worst injustice and the greatest of crimes, as we deduce from the word of Allah:

"Association with [Allah] is truly a huge injustice."

Injustice is not putting something in the right place. And what injustice is more atrocious than to put worship in another place than that which suits it, by dedicating it to a creature (Allah's creation) who is imperfect and incapable of harming or of benefiting itself, and who neither possesses nor the faculty of creating nor of resuscitating?!

What could be more serious than that?! Allah created the human being, but he worships other than Him! He grants him his subsistence, but he seeks it from other than Him! He heals him and yet he asks for healing from other than Him! Is there a greater injustice than this?!

Lesson # 16: Inform the one being guided of the benefits generated by the implementation of orders and the abandonment of prohibitions

The person who learns his religion or the one who is invited to Allah is in need of knowing the fruits engendered by the putting into practice of obligations as well as the harmful consequences of sins so that he can comply with Allah's orders more easily. Indeed, if we inform him of one of His orders, he needs to be reminded of the benefits that flow from it, and when he is informed of the penalty for disobedience, he needs to be reminded of the disastrous consequences that threaten the person who takes this path, and this has been recounted several times in the story of Luqman.

Lesson 17: Advocating to be kind to parents, honor them and respect their rights

We find this in the word of Allah:

"We have commanded the man [beneficence to] his father and mother. His mother carried him [suffering for him] weakness after weakness; his weaning takes place at two years. "Be grateful to Me as well as to your parents. Towards Me is the destination."

This recommendation is of enormous importance, and recommendations are usually made for important things. In this case, it comes from the Lord of the worlds.

It should be noted, moreover, that several exegetes of the Quran have affirmed that His word, "We have commanded man [beneficence towards] his father and mother", is a recommendation that comes directly from Allah, which has been mentioned as a parenthesis in the middle of Luqman's speech.

Thus, we can learn wonderful lessons from these verses, among which the knowledge of the rights of parents, beneficence towards them, kindness towards them, and the discharge of duties towards them.

Lesson 18: Remembering the kindness of our parents helps to be kind to them

Remembering how much happiness parents have brought in the past and continue to bring in the present is also one of the best ways to behave well with them. This will avoid being harmful and breaking family ties.

So meditate on this in His word:

"We commanded man [beneficence to] his father and mother; his mother carried him [suffering for him] weakness after weakness: his weaning took place at two years old."

That is to say: "You the son! Remember all this! Remember your mother's maternal instinct, the pregnancy she had, the way she breastfed you! Remember motherhood, its pains and fatigue! Think about the long time you spent in your mother's womb! Remember you were a heavy load she carried for nine months! Think about the suffering she suffered while standing, sitting and lying down! Remember the pain she endured during childbirth so that you can appear in this life! Think about breastfeeding and all that it involves like pain, fatigue and nights spent watching!"

These are all proofs of generosity, which it is up to everyone not to forget, and to keep in mind at all times.

Lesson 19: Remembering the final destination helps to be kind to them

Among the things that can also help the servant to carry out this divine injunction is remembering the return to Allah. Indeed, the beneficent person towards his parents remembers that he will return to Allah and that he will obtain the reward of his kindness towards his parents and his familial piety, this then increases his motivation to show even more kindness.

On the other hand, the malicious person towards his parents realizes that Allah will judge him and then chastise him because of his bad behavior, so this dissuades him from continuing to commit this sin. We find this in His word: "To Me is the destination."

Lesson 20: A mother's considerable right and her priority right to kindness and good company

We find in a hadith that a man questioned the prophet (peace and blessings of Allah be upon him):

- " O Messenger of Allah! Who is the most worthy person of my good company?"

- He (peace and blessings of Allah be upon him) replied: "Your mother."

- The man questioned him again: "Who next?"

- He answered again: "Your mother."

- He repeated his request: "Who else next?"

- He answered: "Then your mother!"

- He asked: "Who else next?"

- He said: " Then your father!"

Thus, the prophet (peace and blessings of Allah be upon him) mentioned the mother three times in a row because she is the most worthy of good company, and because no one can provide a benefit equivalent to that of the mother, nor approach it in any way.

This is why certain scholars have affirmed that this verse constitutes a proof coming to corroborate and support the hadith of the prophet (peace and blessings of Allah be upon him) in which he quoted the mother three consecutive times. The reason for this is that in this account, Allah mentioned three forms of beneficence of the mother towards her child:

- The first lies in the fact that she is his mother, she is materialized by His word: "His Mother. "

- The second is found in the fact that she wore it: "She carried it [suffering for him] weakness after weakness."

- The third is in breastfeeding: "Its weaning ..."

Neither the father, nor even all those who are kind to the child, were able to endure what the mother suffered. And this requires giving her back good by good and generosity by generosity, and also to consider her as the person most worthy of good company.

But nowadays, it is extremely deplorable to see that some people receive all this continual tenderness and kindness from their mother and that in the end, return this tenderness, kindness and good company to other people, who have not spent a tenth of what their mothers did. They do not live in good company with their mothers and if they have to give time, it is the few crumbs of time they have left.

Is this how we should return good and generosity, and reward benefactors?!

It is for these reasons that harm to the mother is a most serious and blameworthy sin. How can the human being be so bad towards his mother, when she is the one who took the best care of him and honored him?!

Lesson # 21: You can't reciprocate the mother

How much pain and fatigue the mother may have experienced during pregnancy and breastfeeding is in no way comparable to all the good the child could do for her, however great the son's or daughter's kindness and hard work.

Lesson 22: The close connection between the right of Allah and the right of parents

The fact that the right of parents is directly mentioned after the right of Allah indicates its great importance. This proves that after Allah's right, respect for their rights is the greatest obligation. And it is on several occasions that Allah evokes the right of parents directly after His right.

Lesson 23: How to be grateful to parents

Gratitude to parents is expressed by loving them, invoking on their behalf, maintaining family ties and being kind to them.

Lesson 24: The Seriousness of Evil Towards Them

This is one of the biggest and most blameworthy sins.

It is reported in the collections of authentic hadiths of Al-Bukhari and Muslim that the prophet asked three times:

- "Shall I not inform you of the worst of sins (greatest of the major sins)?"

- They replied: "Of course! O Messenger of Allah!"

He (peace and blessings of Allah be upon him) then said: "Association with Allah and being undutiful towards parents." And he straightened up sitting and said, "And to bear false testimony." And he kept repeating that to the point where we thought, "If only he would stop."

Lesson 25: How to behave with parents if they are stubborn or disbelievers

Allah said: "And if both of them force you to associate with Me what you have no knowledge of, then do not obey them; but stay with them here below in a proper way."

Therefore, the child should in no case obey the mother or the father if they order him to associate with Allah or to commit a sin.

At the same time, however, it is necessary to keep them good company.

Lesson 26: The perfection with which the Islamic religion invites to preserve the merits and recognize the blessings

This has been made clear through these verses, by the fact that even when the parents are associators calling for polytheism, Allah commands us to stay with them here on earth in a proper way and treat them with a beautiful conduct.

This is prescribed when they are disbelievers. What if they are Muslims who only order good things and only encourage charity?!

Lesson 27: No obedience to the creature if one must disobey the Creator

Allah says:

"And if both of them force you to associate with Me what you have no knowledge of, then do not obey them; but stay with them here below in a proper way."

Lesson 28: Evil People Put All Their Efforts in Evil

The followers of the error and the false try by all means to spread their falsehoods and to call people to their astray way, as evidenced by the following verse: "And if both force you ."

While at the same time, it is possible that the people of the truth are showing some laxity or feeling weariness about it.

Lesson # 29: The Difference Between Disobedience and Being Evil When Ordered To Do Evil

In fact, many people confuse these two acts by putting them on an equal footing. The fairest advice about this is that there is a difference between the two. Indeed, Allah said:

"Do not obey them" and not "Be evil towards them."

Lesson 30: The merit of the companions and elites of this community

This is taken from the word of Allah:

"And follow the path of him who turns to Me."

In reality, if you consider the situation of the companions as well as that of the elites of this community, you will find that their case is that of those who return to Allah. This is why some exegetes have asserted that the verse: "And follow the path of him who turns to Me", refers to Abu Bakr (Allah be pleased with him). Others claim that it is about all the companions. In both cases, the interpreters of the Qur'an used a method of exegesis which consists in explaining a term by one of its sub-parts or by the best of its sub-categories. This therefore confirms the merit and virtue of the companions and elites of this religion. Therefore, it is essential for us to know their way and to take it. Likewise, we should avoid following a path other than that of believers:

"And whoever splits from the messenger, after the straight path has appeared to him and follows a path other than that of the believers, then We will give him what he has taken, and burn him in Hell. what an evil destination!"

Lesson 31: The importance of choosing friends

Indeed, the believer should not associate with anyone he wishes or desires. Since how much harm is caused by bad company! Thus, a Muslim is required not to surround himself with the first comer, but rather to rub shoulders with virtuous people, as the word of Allah indicates to us:

"And follow the path of him who turns to Me."

Lesson 32: The Merit of Returning to Allah and His Followers

Indeed, Allah has clearly referred to those who return to Him in the above verse. He thus made their way to an example to follow and a way to pursue.

Also, the return to Allah is carried out by bringing together four things:

- Loving Him,
- Submitting to Him,
- Going to Him and responding to Him by carrying out His commands
- Turning away from everything other than Him.

In this regard, Ibn Al-Qayyim (Allah have mercy on him) said: "No one deserves this qualifier except those who combine these four characteristics. And the definition of this term in the pious predecessors went in this direction."

Lesson 33: Actions are recorded

All servant actions are counted. These will be revealed on the day of Resurrection:

"To Me, then, is your return, and then I will inform you of what you were doing."

Lesson 34: Association (associating partners) with Allah is unfounded

"And whoever calls on another deity with Allah, without having clear proof [of its existence], will have to give an account of it to his Lord. In truth, the disbelievers, will not succeed."

Thus, polytheism, whatever form it takes, is absolutely unjustifiable. And this applies regardless of the circumstances or the ways in which it is committed.

Lesson 35: Emphasizes that we will all be resurrected

The *Shirk* (associating partners with Allah) is not based on any evidence, and its followers have no arguments. We deduce that from His word:

"And if both of them force you to associate with Me what you have no knowledge of ..."

When inviting to good or reproving evil, it is necessary to insist on the fact that we will all return to Allah and that He will reward each one according to what he has worked in this life. It's a fact that preachers must consider in their preaching.

Due to its importance, this was repeated several times in Luqman's account:

"Towards Me is the destination."

"Towards Me, then, is your return."

So this is a reality that people constantly need to be reminded of, so that the idea that they will return to Allah and that He will recompense them according to what they have accomplished here below in this world. This should be anchored in their minds, in order that they prepare as they should for the Day of Return.

Lesson 36: The Magnitude of Allah's Knowledge

The knowledge of Allah surrounds everything and nothing escapes Him in the heavens or on Earth:

"O my child, be it the weight of a grain of mustard, at the bottom of a rock, or in the heavens or in the earth, Allah will bring it. Allah is Subtle and Acquainted (All-Aware)."

Lesson 37: The Impact of Faith in the Names of Allah on Righteousness and Works

The more the servant knows Allah, the more he fears Him, seeks to worship Him and refuses to disobey Him. In his recommendation, Luqman repeatedly referred to the names of Allah and His attributes.

Lesson 38: Educate children to be constantly aware of Allah's supervision

For example, if you forbid your child to do something, do not make him care that you are watching him, but constantly refer him to the fact that Allah is watching him. Then say to him, for example: "O my son! Complete the prayer! Stay away from the prohibitions, for Allah sees you, observes you and nothing is hidden from Him! O my son! If you commit even a small sin at the bottom of a rock, in the heavens, or under the earth, Allah will bring it on the Day of Resurrection! O my son! Pay attention and beware of the watchfulness of Allah!"

Lesson 39: On the day of judgment, the scales will be the precision of an atom

Allah said:

"Whoever does good even by the weight of an atom will see it, and whoever does bad by the weight of an atom will see it."

And in Luqman's story, He said: "Even if it was the weight of a grain of mustard ..."

"mustard ...", by saying that, it is indicated that any injustice, however insignificant, will have been accounted for.

Lesson 40: Any mischief will be counted, even if it is in tiny quantities

On the Day of Resurrection, all actions will be exposed, including the smallest. This is why some exegetes have explained the word of Allah:

"Even if it was the weight of a grain of mustard seed", to mean even if it is a tiny unjust act, there will be retribution for it.

This will prove to be very beneficial in the education of children.

Lesson 41: Believe in the two sublime names of Allah: "Al-Latif" and "Al-Khabir"

The two sublime names of Allah: "Al-Latif" (The Subtle) and "Al-Khabir" (The Well=Aware) are jointly cited in many verses of the Noble Quran.

The name "Al-Khabir" indicates that He has knowledge of the most subtle and hidden things, and of those which are obvious and visible even more so.

As for the term "Al-Latif", it has two meanings:
- It has the same equivalent as " Al-Khabir " [And in this case, it is translated as "The Perfect Knower"]

- It means: Allah provides His servants and His allies in such a way that they do not realize it.

Lesson 42: The importance of prayer, the need to perform it and to educate children to perform it diligently

Indeed, prayer is one of the greatest obligations and noblest of duties that Allah has prescribed to His servants. It is the very basis of religion and the most important pillar after the attestation of faith. It is the link between the servant and his Lord.

Also, it is the first thing about which the servant will be judged on the Day of Resurrection. If it is correct, the rest of the works will be, and if it is altered, the rest of the works will be. In addition, it is the criterion of distinction between the Muslim and the disbeliever: to fulfill it is a proof of faith whereas to abandon it is an act of disbelief and excess. Therefore, whoever forsakes it has no part in religion.

Whoever takes care to accomplish it assiduously, it will be a light for him in his heart, in his face, in his grave and in the day when he is resurrected. It will be a door to him on the Day of Resurrection, and he will be gathered there with the prophets, the truthful, the martyrs, and the pious, and what good company theirs is!

On the other hand, whoever does not take care to preserve it will have no light, no argument, no escape on the day of Resurrection; and he will be resurrected alongside Pharaoh, Haman, Qarun and Ubayy Ibn Khalaf. May Allah preserve us!

Lesson 43: Accustom children from childhood to ordering good and condemning evil

This will benefit them, both themselves and others. If the child calls for good from an early age, he will benefit from it and it will be beneficial to others.

The benefit which he himself will enjoy is in the fact that if he invites to good, it will protect him from inciting to blameworthy acts.

There is a saying:

"If you don't call [people to do good], they will incite you [for evil]."

So when the child gets used to calling for good, this in itself will protect him from those who call for evil. In fact, they will consider him as a person calling for good and will find no way to harm him.

As for how others benefit, it is in the fact that it could possibly be the cause of the guidance of some people. And the fact of having been the cause of the guidance of these individuals will fill his balance with good deeds, as the word of the prophet (peace and blessings of Allah be upon him) indicates:

"Allah guiding one person through you will be better for you than owning red camels."

Lesson 44: Encouraging Patience

It is recommended to be patient, especially for preachers and those who command (call towards) good and condemn evil.

Indeed, their occupations require a lot of endurance:

"Endure what happens to you with patience. It is part of the firm resolutions!"

Lesson 45: Followers of firm resolutions

Only strong-willed souls embark on firm resolutions (carrying out substantial affairs).

Lesson 46: The Warning Against Pride and Arrogance

We find this in His word:

"Allah does not like (love) the presumptuous (self-deluded or boastful) full of glory."

Commenting on this verse, Ibn Kathir stated, "The presumptuous refers to anyone who admires himself. And the glorious individual alludes to anyone who boasts of believing himself superior to others."

Lesson 47: Encouraging Moderation

We find this in His word:

"Be modest in your walk, and lower your voice, because the most hated voice is the voice of donkeys."

Lesson 48: Proof that "Love" is One of Allah's Attributes

We find this in His word:

"Allah does not love the presumptuous full of glory."

Lesson 49: Noble behavior

Islamic legislation invites you to adorn yourself with noble characters and warns others against vile behavior.

Lesson 50: Give examples

It is important to illustrate your words with examples when teaching or educating:

"Be modest in your walk, and lower your voice, because the most hated voice is the voice of donkeys."

Indeed, this striking comparison makes us understand that if the fact of raising the voice in an outrageous and disturbing manner had any use, it would not have been a characteristic peculiar to an animal of mediocrity and idiocy who is known to all.

Conclusion

These are some lessons from the noble story of Luqman. Be that as it may, these recommendations that Luqman gave to his son bring together essential wisdoms. Indeed, each of them implies everything that facilitates its fulfillment if it is an order, or else implies everything that helps its abandonment if it is a prohibition.

This illustrates what was mentioned previously in the definition of wisdom, namely: a knowledge of rules with the wisdoms it contains and the discernment that accompanies it.

Luqman, in his recommendations, invited his son to the basis of the religion which is the proclamation of the oneness of Allah ("At-Tawhid") and forbade him association (or polytheism) by exposing him the means allowing one to deviate from this sin.

He prescribed for him beneficence to parents by explaining to his son the means of being kind to them. He enjoined him to be grateful to Him (Allah) and then to be grateful to his parents. Then He decreed a condition which is that they (the parents) do not order him to commit an act of disobedience. And despite this, it is not a matter of being evil towards them, but rather of being benevolent, while refusing to obey them if they force him to associate with Allah.

He gave him the order to regularly remember that Allah is constantly watching him and warned him that he would appear before Him. He informed him that every action he had committed, good or bad, would be revealed on the Day of Resurrection. He forbade him pride and ordered him to be humble. He forbade him arrogance and ostentation and commanded him to be calm and speak calmly. He prescribed him to order good and to condemn evil. He invited him to perform the prayer and to arm himself with patience, acts with which any matter becomes easy, as Allah has affirmed.

So, it is quite worthy that a person who issues such kind of recommendations is called wise and known for it. And the fact that Allah has shown us His wisdom is a privilege that He has granted to him and to all of His servants.

Allah has therefore made the story of Luqman a perfect example to follow.

I ask Allah by His beautiful names and His perfect attributes that He make beneficial what He has taught us and that He make what we learn be an argument for us and not against us.

I implore Him to grant us beneficial knowledge and enable us to do good deeds. I also ask Him to reward Luqman the sage in the best possible way, to forgive him and to wash away our sins.

Allah! Forgive all Muslims, believers, whether they are dead or alive, for You are The Forgiver and The Most Merciful.

And Allah is more Knowledgeable. And may Allah cover with praise and greetings our prophet Muhammad as well as his family and all of his companions.